September 2012

Dear Rick —

I hope your

MEETING BONE MAN

65th year is a

deep joy. I'm

grateful to be

your colleague

Poems by

Joseph Ross

Joseph R

MAIN STREET RAG
PUBLISHING COMPANY
Charlotte, North Carolina

Cover art courtesy of iStockPhoto.com,
layout by M. Scott Douglass

Author photo: Ted Schroll

Acknowledgments

Beltway Poetry Quarterly: "Universal Artificial Limb Company"
Full Moon on K Street (Plan B Press, 2010):
"Universal Artificial Limb Company"
Ibettson Street: "Buddhas of Bamiyan"
Poet Lore: "Darfur 4," "First and Last"
Poetic Voices Without Borders 1 (Gival Press, 2005):
"Buddha Breathes"
Poetic Voices Without Borders 2 (Gival Press, 2009):
"Imagine The Shock"
The Potomac: "Darfur 1," "Darfur 2," "Darfur 3," "Darfur 4,"
"Darfur 5"
RadiusLit.org: "Two Men Raised"
Solo Café: "They Hang from Thick Wooden Pegs"
Tidal Basin Review: "Grieving"
Words. Beats. Life: "Cool Disco Dan 1," "Cool Disco Dan 3"

Library of Congress Control Number: 2012935440

ISBN: 978-1-59948-355-9

Produced in the United States of America

Main Street Rag
PO Box 690100
Charlotte, NC 28227
www.MainStreetRag.com

To my parents:
Vivian Carey Ross and Sam Ross

and always, with love
to Robert

Contents

Part Three: Bone Man Goes to the Beach

Part Four: Bone Man Is Not My Friend

Before you know what kindness really is
you must lose things.

Naomi Shihab Nye
Kindness

Part One:
Meeting Bone Man

Meeting Bone Man

Imagine the Halloween skeleton
of your childhood.

Usually, when you
meet someone,
you extend a hand to touch
living skin to skin.
You exchange a smile,
a pleasantry.

But not with him.
Meeting Bone Man
is not quite like meeting
anyone else.

He may stride
all legs and arms
in your direction
delicately, deliberately.
He may click and slide,
clattering gladly up to you.
He may seem to smile,
toothy and brilliant,
but assign no emotion
to that expression.
It is his only one.
It is the one and true way
teeth fit into the head.
Your teeth look at him
in the same way.
You just don't know it.

When you meet him,
you respectfully acknowledge him
with a nod or note of recognition.
No scream or gasp.
After all, you know
what you are seeing.

You admit him,
you let him in.
There is no point pretending
you have not seen him
once you have.

He may offer you
his spidery hand to shake.
And, he may not.
It is best to follow
his lead.

After all,
touching him
will not change anything.
You need not fear that.
You cannot catch anything
from him.
You already both have
the same condition.
And he knows this.

You look into his eyes,
as is our custom.
But with Bone Man
this will not get you far.
In seeing what looks
like nothing,
he actually
shows you everything.

Bone Man is inevitable.

In the end,
we all lie down in pieces,
in dry and tilting disarray.

Darfur 1: The Boy

My hands move as slowly
as they have ever moved.

I carefully wrap
the stiff, brown body

of this child,
in a bright orange and blue cloth.

A boy, seven years old,
very old, for here.

Elbows, like crickets' legs
teeth, luminous white.

The canvas walls of the tent
gasp for air

as the colored cloth
covers his face.

Darfur 2: The Tent

This tent
seems to breathe.

It inhales quietly:
sucking and hissing and living.

It exhales louder:
hot and sand and canvas.

It breathes
far better
than the seven bodies
I washed and wrapped
this morning,

now lying outside
in the heat
like wood.

I listen for the rumble
of the UN truck
that collects the bodies
each morning.
All I hear now
is the simmering
of sun on sand.

Darfur 3: The Girl

She just appeared
as if by magic,
this girl of twelve or thirteen.

One moment the date palm
stood alone at the edge of the camp.
The next moment,
she stood under it.

Her hands pressed
to her face
in a silent sobbing
we could not stop.

She ate some rice
and cried.
She drank some mineral water
and cried.
She slept for a few hours
and cried.

Tears leaked through her fingers
and carved a path
down the back of her hands.

I never fully saw her face,
her tears, a wedding veil
of untold stories.

She was declared "healthy."
A strange declaration
for a girl, twelve or thirteen,
who has cried ceaselessly
for five days.

The doctor knew
the inadequacy of the declaration.
He wrote:
Visible wounds: none.
Psychological state: mutilated.
Cause of injuries: unknown.

Darfur 4: The Colleagues

We sat in camp chairs with our feet up
in this tent where we also sleep.
It is 2am and for once,
the crickets are louder
than the babies.

Someone got a bottle of wine,
from a visiting doctor, French.

Three of us:
the two with me, my heroes.

Matthias is a genius.
A twenty-three year-old Kenyan
who can organize lines
for food distribution where
no one gets angry
and everyone gets food.

Annette, a forty year-old Italian doctor
who can sew any wound,
calming children while pulling shrapnel
from their quivering legs.

The wine is hot but crisp.
The tent seems to smile around us
as we laugh
and then suddenly stop,
leaning forward to listen intently
to what sounds like horses.

No, we settle back relieved.
It is only machine gun fire
rattling in the distance.

Darfur 5: The Child Soldiers

A German doctor
brought four rescued boy-soldiers
to our camp today,
on their way to the airport.

They are silent and frightened.
They look worn out,
their skin like bark,
resigned and careless.
I only saw the tops of their heads
because they crouched beside the truck
with their heads down
all morning.

Later, I sat with them in the lunch tent.
They ate jello for the first time in their lives.
They did not smile as it jiggled.
Bright red and green cubes
sliding and shimmying
on a paper plate.
What child doesn't laugh
at that?

Outside, after lunch,
the doctor told us
through his optimistic white beard
that each boy had his vocal chords
cut by his superiors.
They were on their way to London
for surgery.
He said none of them
wants to go.

Darfur 6: The Genocide Choir

On this hot night
their voices are bright pinpricks
in a black blanket sky.

Usually, this sprawling refugee camp,
is a planet of sagging heads,
grown accustomed to shocking sounds.

But this always surprises.
These forty or so kids
meet one night a week,

when the electricity works,
and they stun us with singing.
Sometimes a guitar protects them,

usually just their own voices
and skinny handclaps
keep them from turning to dust.

Tonight, they seem wild,
even laughing between songs
as they practice.

Their selections depend upon
who knows the words
and upon who can remember.

Tonight, it's village folk songs
and "God Save the Queen"
until only giggling is saved.

These kids are a shoeless jukebox,
stepping from one glowing star
to the next,

creating a constellation
that arcs across the desert night sky
and never goes hungry.

The Witness Trees 1

I walked with a volunteer into this cemetery,
Seventy years old, he told me.
Been a volunteer here for thirteen years.
Since we buried my wife.
He had skin like brown construction paper
and eyes like blue river stones,
smooth from all that has rushed over them.

He pointed to the place where Lincoln gave
the Gettysburg Address,
that two-minute incantation he hoped
would mend a torn country.

He noted the arcing circle of gravestones,
stitching their moss-covered faces
into a circle deep as death.

He pointed down the hill,
past the spreading rings of gravestones
to where he had relatives buried.
From a Vermont Brigade, he noted.
They lie just beyond that cypress,
a witness tree.
That's a tree that was here even then,
it saw the battle, saw the burials.

He looked at his shoes,
speckled with grass clippings,
their leather quietly torn
from walking with the dead.

He raised his gaze and squinted,
looking down the hill toward the trees.
Them are old trees, he said.
They seen some things.

A Grave Marker at Gettysburg Soldiers' National Cemetery

Gettysburg, Pennsylvania

A cube of stone sits silently,
its granite teeth tight
in this stiff, green place.

The words *Unknown 425 Bodies*
are carved neatly
into its blue-grey face.

It stares up at an angle,
professional, mature, documented.
As if it has just looked

up from its desk,
work still to be done,
buried by eternal tasks.

The original stone
would be furious if it could see
the use the carvers made of it.

It would have strained
and struggled to get away
from becoming

the announcement of this much misery.
It might have thrown itself
into a stream had it known.

This dusted stone
was destined for
a water-goddess' form,

something cool and wet,
curved and delicious
in its desire.

But no, it remains here
in this land of loss,
unable to remember

the names of those it marks,
unable to say their names aloud,
in a voice the living can hear.

Cool Disco Dan 1

Graffiti Artist, Washington, D.C.

Because spray paint smells
like anger,
his name growls
from walls along the train track,

it argues from the trackside
metal boxes restraining
millions of volts.

Would his neon blue name
shock my finger if I touched it?
Would his stylized letters snap
at my hand if I reached out
from my train seat to trace
the artful *Y* of *You can't see me?*

But he is not
an artist, many say.
He is a vandal, a pregnant talent
with an unfortunate disregard
for public property, meaning,
if caught painting he will be arrested
and sent to an art school
behind bars.

Cool Disco Dan and the 21st century
school of train track painters
whose work protests:
End the war now

and *Obama Hates Borf*
and *Sean Taylor RIP*
and *Why So Sad, Ju Ju*?
and *Workers Unite,*

he knows the fatality
of language.
He knows his very name
can be covered over
in one night if
he actually sleeps.

Because of this mortal knowledge,
learned in the dark,
Cool Disco Dan baptizes us
in three dimensional words
so that when we die
our names might be saved too.

Cool Disco Dan 2

You can't see me

Tonight, he hunches
in his too-big jacket,
down Monroe Avenue.

Hooded, his six spider eyes,
constantly on the swivel,
scan everything around him.

He could be going home,
to the club, to a night's work,
or to commit a crime

against an empty space
of cement. His easel:
the concrete canvas soon to be

coated in a turquoise dream
of letters wrapping and rubbing
one another in positions

he was not taught in school.
This is the artist walking,
this is the young man who insists

the mapmakers are wrong.
He breathes here, like the night.
They just can't see him.

Cool Disco Dan 3

Requiem on Cement

In the dark
his hand pulls off
the spray paint can's cap.

He knows this landscape,
by heavy heart.
He drops the cap to the ground

and raises the can
to the exact height
of a fallen boy.

The blue paint stream hisses
until it kisses the wall,
leaving its love

in the tangled letters
of a language known well
to this night artist,

a criminal painter,
for whom stealth
is a color.

He writes the name
of a dead boy
in vivid blue.

The boy, shot and killed
one day ago, lies still tonight
in white, public sheets,

as Cool Disco Dan waves
his painting hands madly
over this concrete clearing,

remembering that sixteen is small,
for a number, and that a name
brings nothing back to life.

The Spirit Boats, Nagasaki

The boats move slowly,
reverent as dusk.

They settle in order
for this solemn procession,

rocking gently
upon these dark waves,

lanterns dangling,
like fireflies

from prow to stern,
casting a dancing reflection

in the worried waters
of this ancient harbor.

Their wooden decks groan
as they try to stay still.

The boatmen whisper,
honoring the journey of wounds

that brings every boat
to this place.

Water slaps each hull
as an innocent reminder

that the river is still
moving, it never ceases

to carry us all forward,
whether we know it or not.

The Universal Artificial Limb Company

The Universal Artificial Limb Company
crouches at the end
of a row of storefronts.
It waits on Wayne Avenue
at the end of a strip mall
whose other stores
are long since closed,
their windows covered
with brown paper and plywood,
like women draped in mourning veils.

Its marketing plan looks like modesty
which these days
does not really sell.

Its name, painted in clean
gold and black letters,
arcs across the front window,
announcing the ancient art
of remembering what has been
dismembered.

Meanwhile, Whole Foods and Starbucks
hover across the street
waiting, plotting, maybe even grinning,
rubbing their manicured hands together
under tasteful signs,
beside stacks of polished fruit
picked by people
who knew what it meant
to bend.

Next door, luxury condos
rise slowly, floor by floor,
a high-rise with the perfect posture
to look down at a store
not even sophisticated enough
to call its product prosthetics.

The Universal Artificial Limb Company
must be careful.
It tries to stay wary,
it tries to deflect the muscled arms
that would shove it aside
in favor of a market more whole,
more hip.
It tries to keep its doors open,
to continue the noble hope of healing
both members and memory.

Part Two:
Bone Man Loves Parties

Bone Man Loves Parties

Bone man sits
on a rich leather sofa,
legs crossed,
watching everyone
in this dancing, drinking room.

He shifts every now and then,
bones rattling and sliding
one against the other.
He's an accordion
of clicks and scrapes,
the glow-in-the-dark
skeleton from childhood's
Halloween parties
come to life.

Though not exactly, to life.
He does live here,
he hangs around a lot, anyway.
Bone man.

Tonight he sits at this party,
in this living room,
turning his skull
toward different conversations
different pairs of breathing people.

I watch him
and turn my own skull
from different conversations

half hoping that he will be gone
the next time
I put down my glass.

But no,
he is standing now,
looking over the shoulder
of a short woman
in a group of three
laughing, well-dressed women.

He watches through gaping
skull sockets of empty eye air.
He listens
through barely-seen ear openings
on each side
of his marbled skull.

He almost seems to smile
since we see all of his teeth.
He nods at the colorful woman
laughing too loudly.
He tilts his head slightly
like he's listening attentively
to the group's thrilling conversation.
Bone man loves parties.

Now he turns again,
shifting his hips and skull,
and crosses the room smoothly.
His femurs and feet

work together perfectly.
Bone Man has style tonight.
He is an orchestra
of extending and folding bones:
Bone Man adapts.

Grieving

Thinking of her
is kind

of a search, a voyage
of looking

for signs and moments,
shadows and gasps

of her. I still
move toward the phone

then stop myself,
a foolish son

who doesn't remember
his mother is

dead. So begins
the search.

A hummingbird
dips into a

blood-colored flower
and I strain

my eyes to search,
to see

the other side
of my breath.

First and Last

Her heartbeat must have been
the first sound I ever heard,

her voice, second, her breathing,
if breath can be a sound.

As she stood at her sink
I lay curled

at the level of the counter,
a slowly blooming boy

within the work that was
the middle of her body.

My voice was the last
she would have heard.

Though the doctor told us
her mind was silent,

I sat beside her bed
on that last morning,

beneath the hovering angels
of ICU machines.

My voice, from outside of her
this time, at the level of her heart.

Of All The Flowers

Of all the flowers
that ring her yard
the camellias were her favorite.
Perhaps because they bloomed
in winter
when she needed them most.

Perhaps they were special to her
because they were
so dignified
so stately
in their restrained pink blossoms.

Unlike the simple daisies
that picket-fence of a flower
all apple pie and white.

Unlike the slutty hibiscus
unashamed red
petals spread wide, drunk
showing everything.

No, the camellias
are roses turned down low,
a simmering beauty.

And still, they bloom
even without her.
This, I suppose
is what pains me.

They are, like her,
clean and simple
slow to open
measured
in their brilliance.

You would think
they could at least
keep a respectful mourning period,
perhaps waiting a year or so
before blooming again.

But no.
On time as ever,
they bloom.

My Mother's Hummingbirds

Their arcs and bolts
of flight and speed
inspired wonder.

How they could hover
just at the lip
of a flower,
touching tongue to petal
in a sweet sip,
humming their zillion
heartbeats a minute,
into frozen seconds of sunlight.

I wonder
if their silvery waiting
was ever freighted with worry
for nest or young or mate?

While they navigated the air
outside her kitchen window
in an unseen whir of wings,
she rubbed her hands,
sometimes raw with worry
in slow, squeezing circles
everyone could see.

Then, her beloved hummingbirds
shot away into the air
like silent stars,
after tiring of the rose

or the camellia,
or the purple sage.

She too, slipped away
in silence,
though she never
tired of anything
that might bloom.

A Man and His Dog

He sat on a bench near the sidewalk,
his ancient dog, in his ancient lap.

They seem to be waiting for a thunderstorm to pass.
He walks this sidewalk daily

in specially-made shoes,
on feet eaten by the tempest of age.

His dog, blind as rain, walks near him,
slower even than he is.

Today, the dog shivers in his lap.
He tells me she has had a stroke.

The dog is shaking, stricken, uncertain as wind.
He seems sad as silence.

I stand still and tell him that I am sorry.
He looks at me, his eyes, two swollen clouds.

His dog stares
into the teeth of the coming storm.

Buddha Breathes

Buddha
breathes in

and every cell
organ and drop of blood
spins and shivers
into
ecstasy.

Buddha
breathes out

and every bone
stone and waiting tear
settles back
into
silky sleep.

Buddha Stands

When Buddha stands
it's his hands

that surround me.
His eyes, those

indifferent coals
only look.

But his hands,
one touching his thigh,

the earth, the grave
that lulls us to sleep,

the other raised
in welcome, in

come and see
what sleeping is

not like
and how restful it is.

Buddha Bends

Buddha bends
to pick something

up from the ground.
Unafraid of what

the dirt might hold,
his eyes land

on something.
His breath is not

held, even
for a moment.

He sees something
but does not

want it.
He has learned

more than that.
So he bends,

in a way that shows
he knows the craft

of bending. His hand
reaches down and

caresses the dirt,
rubs it

adoringly, as one
lover does, carefully

preparing a place
for the other to sleep.

Part Three:
Bone Man Goes to the Beach

Bone Man Goes to the Beach

Bone Man walks
on the beach's bright sand,
shining white as he does.

The sun bangs
on everything today.
Its light is loud.

Bone Man casts a lacey shadow
as the sunlight strains
through ribs and spine.
Everyone squints today,
except Bone Man.

Children play and squeal around him.
They run on fat little legs
to toe-touch the water
only to sprint back,
amazed at the wave's persistence.
Parents guard them carefully.
from a few feet away,
against the water's constant threat.

But Bone Man is relaxed.
He looks out to sea
as if he expects something.
Then he looks down and around
at wild orange beach towels,
women lying with bikini backs untied,
sand-caked little boys

building award-winning canals
making the sea go where they want,
for now.

Through this carnival
of crashing waves and shrieking children,
Bone Man walks.
His grin perfect,
eye sockets taking us all in.

He finds a place
where no children play in the water
and wades in a few feet
until the waves swirl
around his pelvis.
His long, bone fingers
scoop through the water
and suddenly he dips down
and disappears.

The water waits where he dove in
until he re-appears a few feet away
and rises, walking back to the sand.
He stands as the water cascades
from his shoulders,
pouring beautifully down his ribs,
a waterfall of drops streaming
down his bones
to the tips of dripping thumbs.

Washed now,
he continues his slow walk
down the beach.
He threads his way through
frisbees and sand chairs,
giggling girls
and parents carrying babies,
dipping their infant feet
every now and then into the water.

Bone Man watches all of this,
enjoying the intimate relationship
between laughing and drowning.

Two Men Raised

for James Byrd and Barack Obama

A man raised
his hand

to protect his face
from the rocks

on the Texas road where
they were dragging him.

He was tied with chains
to a pick-up truck

and dragged by
five centuries of blind men

who could only see
what they feared.

A man raised
his hand

on a January morning
to swear in public

that he could see
things he did not fear

and that the road
he would walk upon

had rocks
but no chains.

The Young Men Admiring Themselves on the Street Corner

after William Butler Yeats'
"The Old Men Admiring Themselves in the Water"

I hear the young men say,
"'Sup son?" heads nodding
under stocking caps pulled low.
"Same ol' same ol'" they say.
Their faces smooth as sky,
their hands shoved deep
into pockets feeling for
cell phones and the vibrations
of the universe.

They stand on the corner
in a circle of street light
wearing big jackets
on not-so-big shoulders.
They eye each other,
squinting through
cigarette smoke.
They shift
from one expensive shoe to another.

Much of the world's wonder
drifts past these men,
as cars neither slow
nor stop.
But they cannot miss
what they do not see.
So, they stand
on the corner.

An occasional hail of laughter
rises like bullets
from their circle,
but it settles back down,
like a net
over the young men,
pressing them to the concrete,
and the cigarette butts
and the ashes of
this corner
where nothing changes
but the stoplight.

The Silence of Lawrence King

a requiem in two voices

To be a 15 year-old boy is tough.

Man, don't talk to him, he acts like a little girl.

To be a 15 year-old boy
and gay is tough.

He ain't nothing but a faggoty little girl.

To be a 15 year-old boy
and gay and in love with another boy
in your junior high school is tough.

Man, that queer don't know what's going on.

To be a 15 year-old boy
and gay and in love with another boy
in your junior high,
with Valentine's Day approaching is tough.

You got a sweetheart little gay boy?

To be a 15 year-old boy
and gay and in love with another boy
in your junior high,
with Valentine's Day approaching
and ask that boy to be your Valentine is tough.

What did you say faggot?

To be a 15 year-old boy
who is gay, and in love with another boy
in your junior high,
with Valentine's Day approaching
and ask that boy to be your Valentine,
and then to come to school the next day
is to be dead.

Yeah, you can't say shit now, can you?

Imagine The Shock

Imagine the shock
at seeing my name
anger-scratched
on a bathroom wall,
two words small
but deep
slicing steep
carving a canyon
of raw.

They are cut into
green paint
by a furious blade,
a knife-wielding tirade
of pressing, cutting,
crushing, shutting
us down, way down.

It's a simple message really,
these two words
fired bent
as a head hits cement,
followed by the
slow awareness
of spreading pain.
They are mouthed so calmly
from a gun
loaded with only two-words:
"die faggot."

A Nineteen Year-Old Veteran

Make room for the nineteen year-old veteran
rolling his wheelchair down this
immaculate airport terminal hallway,
his face fresh as a high school diploma.

He should be shooting baskets
in a sweaty, screaming gym,
watching a cheerleader
out of the corner of his eye,
and dreaming of wrapping his legs
around her in the back seat of his car.

No such dream today.

But there is plenty of sweat
and more than enough screams
while he dreams of his legs
lying against a broken window
in the back seat of a humvee
in Baghdad.

The Buddhas of Bamiyan

You held your breath
for nearly twenty centuries.

One hundred and eighty feet of sandstone
made you into a standing sand painting

for the wind to frighten away.
In teaching us the impermanence of rock,

you taught us the permanence of fear,
and we have lived here forever.

Your compassionate gaze drifted over
valley and village and river,

a fixed star, a buoy,
in this land of stone.

Your monks lived and slept
in caves that wound all around you.

Here they could
awaken within the image

of the one whose life meant
being awake.

Your grandeur taught us a deep truth:
our beautiful human smallness.

Perhaps this was your downfall,
your silk turning to dust.

They Hang From Thick Wooden Pegs

I. The Prison

They hang from thick wooden pegs
on a white stone wall.
These fire red canvas suits.
Baggy arms, legs, zipper up the front.
Scribbled on the back,
in black-magic marker,
un-erasable, forever: Death-Row.

These suits are shrouds for sure.
A mortician's dream:
cheap, easy, baggy, one size fits all.
No tie-straightening required.

Like a row of red veils
they rest neatly
one after another after another after another.
Silent, creased, still,
the State's will
be done.

Steel crashes on steel
while a guard laughs.

II. The Monastery

They hang from thick wooden pegs
on a white stone wall.
These sun-white cowls.
Wide arms, floor length, generous hood.
They are plain as life itself:
no design, no decoration,
the bearer is the coronation of all that is
simple and focused and feeling
and given over to life itself.
These habits have no mark.
These habits are the mark.

These robes are shrouds for sure.
Only dead men wear these,
only dead men living to please
the One who gave birth to
monks and murderers.
They fall like bridal veils,
peaked, cascading,
a row of warmth waiting
for the one who comes in from the fields,
or the library or his cell.

Silent, creased, still,
God's will
be done.

A sandaled foot jingles
on the church's stone floor.

This Bird

This bird scratches
on the stone window sill,

looking closely at
specks of the world,

trying to distinguish food
from foolishness

and finding it
mostly the same.

This bird, the color
of insignificance,

here off and on
for months,

is gone now,
disappeared

in the blink
of a century.

On Jean-Michel Basquiat 1: Beginning

I thought I was going to be a bum the rest of my life.

He paints us
from the inside

out. From bone
and teeth and

veins like
leashes around

the throat of the
dog that is us too.

He barks numbers
that do not add up,

he scorns the
crown of gold

for a black one,
a shining shadow

in the shape
of everyone.

On Jean-Michel Basquiat 2: Lying

I start a picture and I finish it.

Words cross themselves
out almost as soon

as they are written.
It's not a change

of mind so much as
a lie lifted up to the light,

which is about
to go out too.

On Jean-Michel Basquiat 3: Believing

Believe it or not, I can actually draw.

Christ in agony
shows all his teeth

because this way
we know what

language he
bleeds in.

This way we
know how to

tell cops from
lovers.

This way we
learn to feel

the silky wet
slide of a middle finger

up and into a cheap grace,
a salvation.

On Jean-Michel Basquiat 4: Buying

SAMO as an end to to mindwash religion,
nowhere politics and bogus philosophy.

Samo got something
to sell you.

This cup of salvation
is gold,

is paper, is styrofoam,
but if you love

it enough it
is worth your life.

This mustard seed
smells like a diamond.

This cheek is waiting
to be turned

into wine
but it won't be

because it's getting
a nail pounded

through it,
all so you can

smile with your
bleeding un-turned

cheek and say
Thanks be to God.

I bought what Samo
was selling.

On Jean-Michel Basquiat 5: Dying

I try to think about life.

Palm trees make
lousy crosses,

unless of course
you're smiling

when they drive
the nails through

your own palms.
And if you laugh

while being crucified
you probably have

the wrong idea
about religion.

But the confident and
rhythmic whisper

of waves on sand
can, at times, be

a last anointing,
a sacrament of the

scared, a path through
Times Square

that leads you
to a basement studio

in Abidjan where
a man in a thousand

dollar suit is
painting a backyard

fence brown and
not caring if he

spatters the suit
with his tears.

Did you ever wonder?
Did you ever consider

that being dead is
as drug-free as you can get?

Part Four: Bone Man Is Not My Friend

Bone Man Is Not My Friend

I guess because skin draws
the lines of emotion
he seems pleased enough.

Bone Man never wrinkles his brow
with concern.
His cement-white forehead never creases
signaling irritation.
Those pancake eye sockets
never squint, annoyed or confused
by another's words.
He cast aside
those illusions a lifetime ago.

He is the perfect poker player.
Bone only moves,
it does not reveal.

Teeth line his mouth like seditious books,
stacked straight, untitled.

He survives
in the perfect stillness of bone.
No desert sands shifting.
No ocean waves rolling.

He likes no one,
dislikes no one.
Affection and anger
are myths to him.

They are merely stories
told often
that have never been true.

But Bone Man persists.
Bone Man is.
That is all.

Port-au-Prince, Haiti, 2010

On a photograph by Chris Hondros, 1970-2011, Getty Images

A fence of human hands reaches skyward
grabbing at air, splayed,
dark from the dirty work of dying.

Rigor freezes them
into sculptures that yearn
to speak but cannot.

Their throats have been
filled with bone
and silenced by trembling.

Every now and then
a headlight splashes them
with a beam of white.

When it does
they seem to wave to the living,
a greeting of ghosts.

When the light comes again
you can see the pile
from which they rise.

Twisted shapes melting
and sinking into
an orchestra of decay.

A hundred thousand hands
that once tingled a lover's cheek
or swaddled a wet baby,

now stiffen
in this midnight moment,
straining toward everything.

Before My Father Was My Father

Before my father was my father
he slipped off a sinking ship.
In 1942, in the war waters of the Pacific,
two explosions tore holes
in the skin of the SS Coolidge—
underwater mines,
the captain should have known were there.

This mammoth troop ship shook, shivered,
and then leaned into its own death.
Its yards of steel strained and winced,
shrieking in unnatural directions.

While thousands panicked
my father slipped out a porthole
with a friend who couldn't swim.

He could see Espiritu Santo Island,
and, knowing that a sinking ship
is not your friend, out he went.

He wriggled through the porthole
and then, with chest and stomach
pressing the ship's side,
slid down that vast grey metal wall,
which was slowly flattening itself.

He crawled past welds and markings
which were not intended to see daylight,
designed only for the emerald light
of a drowned world.

He groped his way over thousands of rivets,
and acres of steel, curving and slipping
into their own wet grave.

Finally, he could let go,
and with the SS Coolidge,
he too plunged into the sea.
But unlike the ship, he could swim.
He came back up, tossing water droplets
from his army haircut, breathing,
and splash-walked to the shore
of an island named after the breath of God.

At ninety years old, my father has let go
of wife and home and so much more.
He walks now in the waist-deep waters
of age and quiet, toward an island
whose name we do not know.

Weightlessness

The Buddhist monks
who live next door to my father
bring him a plate of food
every Sunday.
They usually bring fruit,
apples and pears
sliced into smiles,
rocking back and forth on the plate,
a mandala of generosity,
just like the men
who offer them.

Their robes flash orange and brown
as they walk beside
his ivy-covered fence
around to his front door.

Once, when our backyard was filled
with guests after my mother's funeral,
the monk my father knew best visited.
He walked humbly, head down,
into this catholic backyard.
My father beamed,
they hugged, ate,
and the monk sat
for half an hour
talking to the priest,
who hours before
sprinkled my mother's casket
with holy water.

A soothing rain
to a son who fears
dryness.

Months later,
my father planned a visit
to the cemetery.
The monk accompanied him,
gently asking if he might
chant at her grave.
Delighted, my father agreed.

They stood on the brilliant green grass,
over-watered with tears,
while the monk's voice
caressed the cemetery's prickly questions.

His words, moist,
in this buried city of silence.

My Father's Last Friend

He was
my father's last friend.

They drove
around our town,

two old men
with nothing to do

but laugh and eat
and mourn

the world that slipped
in their hands

like a shapeshifter.
They had to stare hard at this world,

forcing their eyes to stay open
so as not to let it out

of their sight,
lest it change

and change again
without their knowing.

At one moment
their world was

made of decades
that suddenly could

dry up into days
and then days that

shrank into hours
and then minutes

that shattered into seconds
which they tried to grab

with their gnarled hands
hoping mightily to save,

at least
the pieces.

But there is
no saving

when you are old;
there is only

laughing, crying,
remembering,

and watching time
become dangerous and small.

On Emptying My Childhood House

The rooms of our house
feel swollen with air.
Its walls once bloomed
with photographs of backyard roses
and a beaming teen
standing beside his first car.
But now, they stand empty-handed,
unsure of where to look.

The ceilings snap with a noise
living people do not make.
It sounds like gone.
It sounds like goodbye.

As I stand in the kitchen
the walls nearly shrug.
They have nothing to say.
They look almost
embarrassed.

Where a living family
once smiled out from wooden picture frames
now only dust frames
guard the faded paint
of these walls.

And these frames,
these skeleton-lines
that took years to be born,
outline photographs of nothing.

These dirt frames cannot be straightened.
They cannot be taken down and saved.
They can only be whisked away
into the empty picture
of air.

Silence

The morning air
seems to have told

the whole house
to hush.

Like we're on a
silent retreat

from dish clatter
and bathroom door snaps.

Only a not-quite hum
seems to rise from the floor,

or a barely hiss glows
from the walls of books,

or immovable regret,
like cut skin before bleeding,

holds its breath in
the rooms where you are not.

Rising at Dawn

Rising at dawn
in my hushed house,
I see from the bedroom window
that the sky is brushed
with the prelude of pink,
the not-quite of light,
still surrounded by the
certainty of darkness.

This faint rose in the night sky
does not bloom,
rather, it gathers shape imperceptibly,
while the persistent night considers
the perhaps of surrender.

It is this most gradual approach,
this silent other,
that changes everything into
the almost of hope.

When The Dead Stand Up to Sing

When the dead stand up to sing
they clear their dusty throats,
remembering a song they learned long ago
when breath actually flowed through
their beating bodies.

Today they stand to sing,
not in their own world of damp and darkness
but in mine.
They are a surprising choir, for sure,
row upon row of stony singers,
heads thrown back,
mouths open wide as water.

They pull air into skeleton lungs
from all sides and they sing it out
the same way.
First quietly, then stronger,
a melody that rises and falls
like they did:
without warning.

Their choral sounds layer each other
like graves,
their notes slip in and around each other.
They are dense, with barely enough space
to breathe.

Their song is sometimes hope
and sometimes horror.

At one moment their voices
are bright, like light.
At the next, they drop like darkness.
These singers have fallen and risen,
they have come through
and come out.

This skinless choir stands always ready
to sing its searing notes,
while I wish, in my childish way,
for the piercing hope that their song
will come to an end.

But no. Their song is not
of blood and breath.
It cannot just stop
like those things.

Their song is of victory.
Their song is of overcoming.
It is not the music of ashes,
clinging to us all.
It is the music of light
breaking through every crack
in every stone.

This is not a lamentation, damn it.
This is a love song.
This is a love song.

Chris Abani
from "Sanctificum"

Gratitude

I am grateful to many people for helping to bring *Meeting Bone Man* to publication:

Randall Horton, without whose encouragement and support this book would not be in your hands. E. Ethelbert Miller for friendship. Naomi Shihab Nye for kindness. Jericho Brown for practical help and laughter. My American University colleagues and students, especially poets David Keplinger and Kyle Dargan whose advice helped to shape this manuscript and whose friendship I treasure. Naomi Ayala, Rose Marie Berger, Sarah Browning, Carmen Calatayud, Niki Herd, Melissa Tuckey, and the members of D.C. Poets Against the War. Michael Cahir and my colleagues and students at Archbishop Carroll High School in Washington, D.C. Kevin A. Nelson II, a former student and poet who I wish were alive to read these poems. Michela Costello Lakkala, Fred Joiner, Melanie Henderson, Katy Richey, Sue Scheid, Peter Montgomery, Dan Vera, Jody Bolz, Truth Thomas, and Katherine Howell for their helpful suggestions. Jefferson Pinder for the friendship that shares families. Dr. Sharon Locy and Sr. Teresita Fay, RSHM who taught me to love poetry at Loyola Marymount University in Los Angeles. My family: Sam & Vivian Ross, Gina and Rick Meng, Melissa and Dave Wilson, Caitlin, Shannon and Laura Meng for encouragement. Robert Waxman, for everything.